GLADLAND

GLADLAND

SUSAN BRADLEY SMITH

RECENT WORK PRESS

Glandland
Recent Work Press
Canberra, Australia

Copyright © Susan Bradley Smith, 2020

ISBN: 9780648685340 (paperback)

 A catalogue record for this book is available from the National Library of Australia

All rights reserved. This book is copyright. Except for private study, research, criticism or reviews as permitted under the Copyright Act, no part of this book may be reproduced, stored in a retrieval system, or transmitted in any form by any means without prior written permission. Enquiries should be addressed to the publisher.

Cover image: by eduardo cgf on unsplash.
Cover design: Recent Work Press
Set by Recent Work Press

recentworkpress.com

PL

For Peter & Martin, two drummers who died together on the road to a Byron Bay gig in 1981, and for my father (who sadly policed their tragic accident) Colin Leslie Smith, 1941-2019.

May you rest in peace.

Contents

1: LAMENTATION LAP DANCE

Nancy with the staples in her stomach	5
Those boys, all those boys	6
Hamburger joint, Detroit	7
In New York	9
Louisville, Kentucky, I love you so	11
Feeling American baby	12
Things Italians invented that aren't on the tourist map	13
Failing to be Anita Garibaldi	14
Tuesday has no name for Thursday	15
Tonight I will write my last letter to you	16

2: PRAISE PONY

You promised me the future you did	19
When smoking and soirees fail to fascinate	20
Inside your hair	21
The poet who died for your phone	23
Waiting for my blind date, thinking about you	24
Calm, calm intelligence	26
That field of horses	27
Girlhood, guns and you	29

3: CONSOLATION CONGO

Oh to be a murderess, tra la li, tra la lum	33
The lifeguard is taxed	34
Breeding ground	35
Axe: for ice	36
Trying for love on the telephone	37
Departure, soon	38
The sonic life of tennis	40
Debriefing	Happy	41

Coastal fugue	42
Selling the surfboards	43
Glamorous discontinuum	45
Afterword	46

All of our lives now (all of our lives)

Till the end of time (end of time)

Because this love now (because this love)

Is only yours and mine (yours and mine)

Hush sing 'Glad All Over' (1975) by Dave Clark & Mike Smith (1963)

The Glam Descend is my musical term for those great descending guitar-led 70s hits... But its roots come from the Druidical curse known as the Glam Dicenn, in which the poet stands on one leg, screws up one eye and extends one arm and delivers a mighty poetic blow to his opponent. As the Oxford Dictionary of Celtic Mythology comments: "The victim of the Glam Dicenn would be shunned by all levels of society." I have incorporated this idea into my work in order to show the power of the once-outsider both in terms of the poetic Glam Dicenn and the musical Glam Descend.

Julian Cope, *Head Heritage*

1: LAMENTATION LAP DANCE

Nancy with the staples in her stomach

Your daddy is Frank Sinatra, and even though
he was the kind of man who organised poker
parties in Vegas with scotch on the table and
whores beneath, blowing the players, it was
you who earned the sin in your surname
by posing naked for Playboy. Please Forgive
Me Daddy, you crooned, wearing your
perfect patent leather boots that never left
the runway, squashed a fly. America is full
to the dead-fish gills with women like you,
with eyes like yours, opaque with a future
that never arrives because you took
the bait. Elsewhere, everywhere maybe,
women eschew your entrepreneurial guts,
yet listen to your records, same sugar in our
veins, same metallic centerfold pain in our bellies.

Those boys, all those boys

I said a prayer for you and it went to
                        Glastonbury, got lost, stole
money to get home. America is dropping
                        not acid but, with septic hearts,
                        BOMBS
                        everywhere, but mostly not on
white Christian people & watch out just
                        WATCH OUT
                        suburbia is losing its sex appeal
and the moon has no name for planet earth
                        we are just a drag
even the record player knows it is spinning lies
                        but you love me forever
                        I AM YOUR BABY
there we go now: there we go.

Hamburger joint, Detroit

We are so drunk. We are so
very drunk. You have ordered
for me because I am so
drunk I can barely speak
but if truth be told we are in
good form compared to the
other patrons. The other patrons
are shooting up in the booth
behind us. I am at least not
falling off my barstool like
the woman to your left, she
has really lost her shit, lying
there on the cold floor like
one of Caravaggio's sluts. Our
waitress is not like in the movies
at all, she is a fierce ringmaster,
she tells me I need fries and
I do. I really need fries. My
hamburger is the biggest
hamburger in the world, I am
going to marry this hamburger
because you, my friend, married
some other girl, some other
girl who does not get so very
fucked up, and is an even
cheaper date. Some dude
pulls a gun and we leave,
laughing all the way home.
For some reason I am still
hungry, hungry as a mama
pig, but you're done playing
with me, you go upstairs to
your sleeping-beauty wife
leaving me to begin a romantic

relationship with your pantry.
I take my panties off—my
signature move thanks to
the sex scene in *Jaws*—and
reach to the top shelf for
the honey that will kill the
world. My underwear is
on the floor, wet from the
reliable migration of tears.

In New York

I saw your friend Matt
take his clothes off in a play
you lived in St Marks Place
where downstairs hat makers
stayed opened all night
what for I asked do they deal
drugs too but all their
goods were velvet, soft as
as ocean moss, and I bought
a red and white striped Cat-
in-a-hat Dr Seuss number
for my crazy husband who
wore it without irony and
a floppy green beret for
me, she who had a thing
about the military going
soft or not soft enough—by
the way does Switzerland
truly have a navy? I was
pregnant. I ate lots of
melted cheese sandwiches
while you were at work
being a famous young
editor in a high, high rise
building. You taught me
a lot including the value of
a good manicure and how
to talk to clients from the
South—who doesn't want
to discuss what they ate
for breakfast? I slept a
lot and listened to your
fish tank bubble. I caught up
with Charlie and Amy we had

hamburgers in an empty
diner then we said see you
later but we didn't—I caught
a Pan Am plane to Sydney
but got off in Hawaii because
leaving America was too
hard and I missed the ocean.
I phoned you in New York
your friend the miserable
teacher answered and was
rude she said you were at the
drycleaners getting a cigarette
hole in your new dress invisibly
mended then you came on the
line and said to me don't worry
go home give birth in Australia
your daughter will always know
who she is and years later I said
the same sentence to you with
a monstrous lack of foresight.
When you think about it, it is
amazing we still talk to each
other. Now you live in Bristol
and I live in Perth clearly we
both remain slightly stupid,
our daughters far less so.
We never discuss
New York.

Louisville, Kentucky, I love you so

Surrounded by three-year-old
thoroughbreds and Mint Juleps,
dreaming of bourbon and sugar
and rose-petal-woven blankets,
other things unsilken that happened
included well I've plumb forgotten
but it involved money and drugs
and t-shirted promises *will work
for weed* and women and loose
sex in long toilet queues and
love squandered like a lottery
win I can't really remember
much else after going to the
Member's Stand to watch the
wrong race which has become
a metaphor for my entire life,
my entire goddamned life.

Feeling American baby

I first saw the Pope in Detroit,
he was in his Popemobile looking
like he was auditioning for a role
in the Jetsons I was in a Polish
neighbourhood in Detroit did I say
I was in Detroit, that forward-thinking
Motherfucker of a place in the only
restaurant that was open eating
food that was very white-coloured,
strange food for a black town, and
outside aside from the Pope convoy
was this boy, I kept seeing him, the
same cute boy in the same jeans,
looking at me like I was a recipe
without a book to be ripped from,
he looked like a movie star,
no one bothered to tell me
America was scratch and smell,
I had to figure that out myself,
also the answer is lemonade.

Things Italians invented that aren't on the tourist map

Testaccio is a fun suburb. The river licks its lip
at one edge, at the other the dead poets lie and lie
and lie together in the prettiest cemetery in the whole
wide world. At the spinal bottom of this postcode
is a mountain of shards, mercantile remains of giant
terracotta bulbs, once oiled, once wined, now just
antique rubbish. And right here is a defunct abattoir,
now University of the Arts, crime site extraordinaire.

Here, just before Hitler began his blitzkrieging, two
men carried out a series of experiments worthy of
NAZI citizenship—they induced seizures in the
soon-to-die cattle by the application of electric
shocks. By the next decade this talent had been
imported to England and America and the
recipients were now human, and the application
was unmodified, and soon Sylvia was letting us
know what it felt like to have ECT without
muscle relaxants, without hope or oil or wine.
It was all just a gothic novel: crime unknown.

You can stand in the very spot these boys made
good, made the future more convulsive. I expect
they were pretty excited. I feel a bit sick, and make
for the vegan café across the road at the markets
but only get as far as the first bar. The world is full
of smart venues and stupid men. It really is.

Failing to be Anita Garibaldi

Ana Maria de Jesus Ribeiro da Silva, your statue kills me. Comrade-in-arms, Romantic revolutionary, *You must be mine*, Garibaldi whispered to you, and you became his, fighting together until the end. What a horsewoman you were, the plains of Southern Brazil giving your hips their gaucho waltz, still seductive after four children. He was—do not spit at me—a womanizer, your red-shirted man. Did you think about this as the dogs mined you from your hastily-dug, shallow grave, or as he wore your striped scarf hailing the new king of a united Italy? Or, later, when Mussolini erected this statue in your honour on the Gianicolo? And there you remain, on your rearing horse, a baby pinned to your breast like a medal, a pistol in your hand. Sometimes we just shoot the wrong people.

Tuesday has no name for Thursday

It is only natural that I think about you here,
in the city where we met. The only declared
bond between us is friendship, but that word
'love', I'd drink it if you said it, even if it were
petrol, even if I would die soon afterwards.
Then you say it. At Fiumicino Airport I feel
like I am leaving with your ghost. I am
incredibly anxious, alien to myself, and
unheeding of your own corrosive protests
against yourself. Waiting to pay for coffee,
women around me stare at packets of
cigarettes they will not buy. Some lick
their lips. Men avert their lonely eyes from
magazines. Hypershine is everywhere, yet
none of us are reflected. I get useless coins
for change. We board different planes,
you fly to Honolulu, I eventually arrive
in London. I am wearing your lips, your skin,
I have stolen your eyes, I do not match
my passport, I am deported. As if you
were America itself, you have trusted
in my sure surrender.

Tonight I will write my last letter to you

It will be short and full of lies,
although butterflies will swarm from my mouth, betraying
me. You will read this letter in bed with your pregnant wife
because you said to me Don't ask me to be the man who
does that. Are you making her scream with your complicated
heart? You flirted and fucked with me like Theocritus,
snagged my soul, promised truth but forgot that some
would rather die before yielding to passion. You have
left me naked, turned me towards my own wife-life, choked
me with photos of my children in your hands. That was
after you dragged me backwards by my own hair to bed,
cried about your mother, read from your new book, shook.
So tonight I will write my last letter to you.

2: PRAISE PONY

You promised me the future you did
for Sylvia Plath (1932-1963)

One of you was bound to get bored with the other: two writers in love, we've all seen the end of that movie. Except you, perhaps. For a woman so well-versed in the Classics, it was a dull surprise to watch you marry your father, and build a life that was stuck in the decade of gloom and gloss and atomic fear and post-war appliances that did not yet include Valium or vibrators. You braided your hair and rugs, you failed to remember your beginnings, you believed babies were the logical produce of love, and that marriage (after the fall) was a business, grinding out the future. You forgot to awake each morning wound by love, in need of him blowing you a fresh membrane, too ready to play secretary and house, to be everybody's best girl. You burst. Without skin, you bled and wrote and you stung. You had just begun. You stayed too raw even for the touch of daffodils. Stupid woman. We needed you more than him. Christ oh Christ of the post-Christian heart: you had just begun.

When smoking and soirées fail to fascinate
for Rosemary Tonks (1928-2014)

All of your Februaries were full of draughts and cracks and
your summers shocked and satiated with volte-face—
weary with tripped dedications you glided from
one life to another, from fame to extreme religiosity and
retreat, like an ocean floats itself from Asia to Africa
only to evaporate to an Amazonian afterlife. Your
brokenness is our Iliad; your rejection of us our
Odyssean challenge. Unless—you said it—we are
not people but mattresses, the very mattresses we
lie upon. You, knowing this, burnt everything.
You left the party.

Inside your hair

for Dorothy Hewett (1923 – 2002)

> *'I have known the tuck-in of a child / but inside my hair waits the night I was defiled'*—Anne Sexton 'Angel of the Love Affair'

Smooth utopia is melting all over me. The list of things I'm not allowed to enjoy anymore is growing daily, and includes Woody Allen films because Woody upgraded a parental baseball outing into having an affair with his partner's daughter which is not very cool. Also on the list: Gary Glitter. And now, since your daughters' confessions, you too. You are top of my pops. Feminist goddess of my youth, mouther of mantras that reminded us to *live live live* so we did not die with nine-tenths of our tremendous worlds still inside our heads—you betrayed us all. Basically, you were your own cult. Sexual liberation and freedom for women: who can argue with that? And who wants to look at the fine print of that agreement, or indeed fight with any glamorous communist? Your daughters lived that life with you. 'Do you want to fuck my daughter?' you'd say, in your bohemian way, and someone at the dinner table would always oblige. Childhoods spent as party favours, nubile jailbait, your parental maladministration cannot be rewound: you grew them up fast, you grew them up hard, but was it emancipation or collective regression? It was an ordinary story, in that we all know that louche plot, and the churn of its ever after. They felt loved by you they said, despite everything. It was the 1970s. It was borderline OK. Teenage groupie Lori Maddox was after all giving it up for Jimmy Page—by all accounts they were in love. Why not? Thirteen-year-olds know all about that. Just ask Romeo and Juliet. And herein lies the problem: literature provides a pedigree for such liaisons—not to mention rock and roll, which cradles our own deceits and peddles them back to us as gospel. *Do you wanna touch? Yeah! Do you wanna touch me there?* Our relationship to the monstrous is selective, only vaguely monitored by law. You've rendered the holy unholy, even worse, you're John Donne in reverse. Your daughters are in pain, and me too, and you are a star, and your writing is beautiful, it has always been, will always be, a cut-glass clarion call to a better life. But the hurt of you is prehistoric. *Friday night no one in sight and we got so much to share.*

So, I have one question to ask: when was shopping your daughters for sex ever a good idea? And how much had you had to drink? Sorry, that was two. But fuck you.

The poet who died for your phone
for Xu Lizhi (1990-2014)

You'll never be as famous as your own headline. I'd never even heard of you, to my shame. I apologise for the baroqueness of indifference which plagues us all. It was time for me to read more Chinese poets—as though you were a category in a department store—and I came across a blog about your death. I'm impressed: you jumped from the seventeenth floor of a Shenzhen mall. Zola wrote kindly and fondly of malls. Extraordinary, what some will champion. But I feel for your predicament: I too was once an economic migrant, and it is an experience that is arctic to the soul, earning money for pigs. I understand you made electronic components for a Taiwanese company that made phones for us Western consumers? Yet you, *dagong shiren*, migrant poet, wrote and wrote between shifts until you climbed and jump and flew, having done with your running along railways to cities and other imagined futures. Who were you, really, before you traded in your youth, your muscle? What would you have written for your own dating site profile? I wish we had met, and shopped and eaten and laughed. Maybe—afterwards—even jumped together.

Waiting for my blind date, thinking about you
for Robert Lowell (1917-1977)

The London sky this afternoon is alcoholic—golden and dangerous, perfumed by bedlam. In New York the sky films New York stories, like yours. You died in a taxi that had driven you from JFK Airport to West 67th Street, just off Central Park. You were returning from Ireland, having just left your third wife, off to visit your second. Tell me, how do hearts feel about being attacked? And do taxi drivers take the rest of the day off after such an incident or do they not bother? Cal, you hard-drinking glorioso, you monster, you emperor, you tyrant—why were you clutching so furiously in your arms that painting of your wife? Your dead-man's limbs had to be forcibly broken to wrest that stringed, brown-papered, jetsetting parcel from your grip. Needs must. I'm looking at her now, your last wife (subject, model, muse, marrier of mad painters and poets): 'Girl in Bed' by Lucien Freud. The National Gallery is hung with secrets, they swallow them, they declare them lacunar, nail them to walls of varnished vernix, keeping them alive, if silent. *I will eat you for breakfast, drink you for dinner, kill you for bedtime*, says the girl in the painting. If I was that girl, if I had been Lady Caroline Blackwood, I'd do it all again. I know. I'd do everything again, from the sable to the hogshair to the sawn-off arms: oh, to be held so fast, so tight, painted so bright, that is a commonwealth to die for. Meanwhile, I'm waiting for my date. I'm bothered. But my shoes—high-heeled pumps, *shiny shiny, shiny patent leather*—make me happy, marking the floor with important pecks as I move from portrait to portrait. I amuse myself wondering of each: would I kiss them? All the while I can feel the onset of panic at being alone and in public, I am honey turning to comb. I am, it seems now, always alone and waiting—how must your ex-wife have felt, when you failed to arrive? Volcanic, ready to Pompeii you, I presume. God, please bless my life with such geology, and memories stronger than sandstone.

PS My date has not shown up. I can't stop thinking about you. If you could have, you would have written about your own death. It was as you'd've wished, in some regards: natural, no teeth on the ground or blood about the place. Things I need to know before grief eats me alive: is that what men really want, to return to their ex-wives? Had you been kissing the painting? Does the past taste of turpentine?

Calm, calm intelligence

for Dorothy Whipple (1893-1966)

Your final novel broke my heart: 'A very good novel indeed about the fragility and also the tenacity of love' wrote the *Spectator* in 1953. It was then spectacularly ignored for fifty years. I love the way you wrote 'fairly ordinary' tales about the destruction of a happy marriages, yet they are not—ordinary—each tragedy wears unique (if mass produced) shoes (it is the wearer, and her own ankles, that make such claims), and each demise of love makes for compulsive reading. I like your characters, they are what I have always (unfashionably) wanted to be: that strange creature, a happy housewife. Still, disaster will strike, and it is often spelt 'MAN' and reads something like 'Husband, in a moment of weak, mid-life vanity, runs off with a French girl'. Dorothy, you superb stylist, you of the calm intelligence and the preoccupations of a Midlander: you entrance me with your simple prose and spot-on psychology. 'We have all delighted in this unjustly forgotten novel; it is well written and compelling.' Some were made into films. You were married a long, long time. You died. Did you also make jam?

That field of horses
for Anne Sexton (1928-1974)

I'm buying a new car today, a Ford Mustang, to honour you, but also to own my own horror story. Is that too gruesome? Like renovating your kitchen with a modern gas oven in the suicide-vintage style of Sylvia's 1963 Primrose Hill flat? The things that mothers do to their children is monstrous, and reciprocated, revenge like reflux. But oh my, how you do inspire: your holy disgust with destiny, your life trapped like a finger in a slammed door, your howling, your words hurting just like the angels injured Lucifer—until one day you just had no tricks left. Although your car did: it had an exhaust pipe which smoked not peace but carbon monoxide, and a home called garage, which became your earthly vault. I stand in the showroom with a sympathetic salesman who says he'd rather be surfing, but is not truly envious of my freedom to purchase or roam—that he is grounded and cherished and loved is as obvious as morning. He moves to open the Mustang's door for me to imagine life afresh, become its owner, its new rider. I become the car. There is no choice left but colour. Because carboxyhemoglobin has a characteristic cherry-red colour, because it turned your skin the palest pink and your lips the brightest, most errant red, and because all our choices are made from the remnants of the choices we've made before and you already chose red, fast cars, fur coats and nakedness before you chose gas, I can't rest with your primary pick. I choose cyanosis blue instead, because that did not happen to you, that suffocation-blue, but say, politely, to my salesman, 'Pacific Blue, please'. Apparently, though, that's not an option, my attempt to enter his world abruptly rebutted: I can have Deep Impact Blue or Kona Blue or Azure Blue or Bright Atlantic Blue or Grubber Blue or Gulfstream Aqua Blue, or nothing. Asphyxiated by possibilities, I am. What happened to Nightmist Blue? 'Give me what you've got'—no more smiles from me—I say, and end up with floor stock. Blue is Blue. Most men are born as blue as babies, you need to check their soles lifelong for danger signs: this, women only sometimes know. I thank you Anne, as I drive out and away and up, winding myself along highways to rough fields and wild losses and cliffs that make you feel as alive as an apple. I thank you for the fast impress, for the reminder that women and cars are created from forged metals and we are therefore built for the thrills that come between living and dying. In one single gesture, you both defeated and succumbed to mortality. As for those of us left in your wake, well—I am still looking for a better place to be a brumby.

Girlhood, guns and you
for Meherun Nesa (1942-1971)

1
Today, according to the tabloids, Dhaka is a dysfunctional megacity. The drains in this mighty capital can't cope with monsoonal flooding. In the 1960s the city worked, but what worked for six million people doesn't for seventeen, so I don't drink the tap water, not even for solidarity. The Chinese have done a billion dollar deal for a Dhaka to Chattogram high-speed train. The rice crop is set to hit eighteen million tonnes, above target, yet one-and-a-half million bank accounts have been closed by unhappy citizens. Everywhere, a crush of hope and filth.

2
One dark night in March of 1971 Operation Searchlight began its killing. Nationalism (bad luck) is such a cultural thing, what with its shouting intellectuals and poets and Language Movements. Bang bang bang went the Pakistani guns. Bangladeshi writers and academics were taken blindfolded to torture cells, then executed. Revolutionaries do not kiss the enemy. *Kill three million of them and the rest will eat out of your hands.* Poverty is a flame-shaped harridan, but she was never the main event.

3
I write to you, dear Meherun Nesa, daughter of the British Raj, to say sorry. I'm glad the 1960s were good for you, you trailblazer, copywriter, Philips Radio company girl. The odd spot of family financial insolvency had not stopped you writing Bangla poetry for a decade before graduating to mass uprising participation and hoisting of the Independence flags on your roof which sadly led to your murder alongside your mother and brothers. Still, your murderer was eventually hanged, and a stamp with your face on it was released. Documentaries were made. But I don't need to tell you your own pro-liberation story: *our demands must be met.* Amader Dabi Mante Hobey.

4
Did you feel your body being chopped into pieces and cubed and moved, like trying to solve a problematic sestina? Even that is a PG version of events. Real story goes: bullet in stomach head bashed on floor raped then gang raped to death last penetration being a bayonet skewered body parts thrown from soldier to soldier (sport). Who can remain steady, knowing this? *Our demands must be met.* Amader Dabi Mante Hobey. For you, for this, I will always pray, to that bitch, the moon, who does nothing.

3: CONSOLATION CONGO

Oh to be a murderess, tra la li, tra la lum

You ran into me bodysurfing. You were made of thunder and mirrors. You marshalled me to safety, the shark alarms sympathetic to your cause. You smelt faintly of salt and horror movies, lurking there beside the lifeguard, who declared me unharmed. You knew everyone on the beach. Your message transferred into me as if by gravity, like ink from a punctuating cartridge. You said you had a spare beachside apartment to rent (you owned the building) and a wife at home you'd like me to meet. You lied. You stood blocking your door, nagging for my number. You grew taller than your chandelier's talons, rounder than your cellar's aged barrels. You forced a pen upon me, *I only want your number*, a beautiful combination of physics and chemistry and engineering. I began to write on your grocery list which included garlic and nappies. Your hands were too soon filthy with rape and seed to fend off the nib and knob and mouth and thrust tube that prefaced your shroud. You were my uncles, the hand over my primary mouth, you were the bastard at every barbecue in history, the flasher in the church, the man in every dark. You were a poem I wrote with a cheap hotel pen instead of re-enacting your sad opera for the police. I liked the sounds of you both, your click, your clack, your leak of Chartres-blue blood. Your fatal snap.

The lifeguard is taxed

Her drowning was stranger than the story of Eden. She's on the hard sand now, waiting for the emergency services to arrive, but there is no doubt she's dead. Her ovaries are sodden orchards, her lungs choked billabongs, separated twins. The lifeguard who is really a very nice kid, he is, wishes he'd had the courage to ask her out when the chance still pumped blood, even pulled the maid into the cool cement chamber of the surf club house and made love to her liked he'd wanted to. Counterfactually, the sandbank would then have collapsed without her, she'd be no sad mermaid with that hair wrapped around her dead, green throat. Someone had pulled her down, he swore, but no one believed the lifeguard, perhaps it was sunstroke talking. Zinc can only achieve so much in terms of protection. You are a peach, girl, he'd thought, watching her enter the water, You are made entirely of fruit—then felt ashamed of his own poetry. Now, he is angry, and will never again be so stupid as to ignore the gods. He returns to the lip of the ocean, and has a quiet word with Poseidon, in the Australian way which involves much silence and no mucking about.

Breeding ground

The Indian Ocean across the road is showing her breasts to
the moon. The butter next to my bread is packaged like
gourmet soap. It has been cultured and churned by Pepe who
is otherwise a stranger to me, like everyone here. I am not
the only person dining alone, though I am certain to be the only
guest sleeping at the grimy backpackers that promised so
much but is full of miners and captured travellers and women
even sadder than me. All this I can cope with but not the
table at the window, not the mother and her two children who
make me think about Durkheim and the ethics of suicide.
They are squabbling over the desert menu where the dishes are
named after seductive colours coupled with Aboriginal place
names. Cottesloe by night is full of the kind of fun that true-
hearted police officers know all about, the crimes of the rich
being that much more squalid than credited. And here they
are, out from the zoo of their home, debating the virtues
of New York as though they were citizens of global decency.
There is hope, perhaps, for the son—he refused to sing Happy
Birthday to his sister (it was her sixteenth) because she was
a fucking bitch. Clearly, because her absent father had just
phoned mentioning her present, the sum of which deposit
she had gleefully declared, winning the battle for favourite,
so it seemed. The mother rumbled her purse for pills, and
tissues; the fatherless waitress blew out the candles, teary,
considered using her degree to negotiate a peace treaty.
All players fondled their phones. This meal, this horror, this
is the circus-ring of all women who dare to mate with different
beasts. And look at the mess: the loneliness: the desolation:
the cracked winter light against the startled window, witnessing
it all. Thank you Daddy, thank you so much.

Axe: for ice

My life is leased. The front door is off its hinges, hanging like a hooker against exhausted bricks. Android calm, I walk into my home. I spy the burglar, busy pissing on my new sofa. He hits me over the head with my microwave and I fall in a wet mess to the floor. His accomplice shouts from upstairs 'Rich Fucking Bitch' then slides down the bannister like a wicked child. His jeans have a rip in their seat. No underwear. The indecency of everything—of my unkind work; of my girlfriend's son-in-law who'll soon joke 'You'd've loved it' when we say *At least we weren't raped*; of the reality that I'm not on the drugs that killed River Phoenix; in fact the entire list of all my good-girl bourgeois graspings and exertions (*such* a pretty home)—all these unbecoming, unseemly, rude contracts of the soul suddenly leave my body. They form a hovering mass of ghostly chunder before my eyes, a spiritual tomahawk with an undecided swing: who deserves to live or die? Later, the police will tell me 'Thirty break and enters already tonight' (it's only been dark an hour) and 'Ice epidemic' and 'You can fill the forms of loss in online.' But for now I have forgotten how to speak or spell or cry or claim. I wretch upon the floor as the men, swagged-up, flee. Justice becomes me. Just as I'm all Ophelia-in-the-river, I begin to breathe again. I gather my garlands, and wonder ridiculously if they have taken my Easter eggs. Because I am so hungry, I am my only agent, I am both bed and flower, sowed and reaped, and I have much work to do. Especially
regarding ~~revenge~~ love.

Trying for love on the telephone

'His name was Honey,' I said, the
Australian journalist on Fleet Street
who'd convinced King George that
silence and remembrance was a
good publicity stunt. 'Besides,' I said,
'it's only 8am here on the west coast
of this vast colony that irritates you so'.
If we keep this conversation up
there'll be silence rocking all over
the world. Like the helicopters
this morning, protecting Prince
Charles and Camilla and their pretty
poppies on their visit to the not-Scottish
Perth. 'It was like Vietnam out there
by the Swan River this morning,'
I said, feeling stupid, just stopping
myself from pushing the metaphor
north of Capricorn, to our current
apocalypse: him, there; me here.

Dry toast makes a lot of noise when
crunched but is a kinder sound no doubt
than the collapse and crush of bones in
coffins. Never a monarchist before
sundown, 'Fuck the Royal Family,'
he offered, then, 'My all-time favourite
Gibson Les Paul guitar's colour is
called Honey Burst'. This, just as I'd been
about to say goodbye. Which I soon
did, grateful for our fresh armistice.

Departure, soon

The flight had been long delayed, and now it was the hour of moonspeak, when waiting passengers cast no shadow as they sauntered barwards to this and that terminal DELIGHT. One man in a high visibility vest fresh from the mines tripped over either his WITHERED soul or an underfoot, landmined, carry-on bag, and fell onto the breasts of the closest, most careless woman. They laughed like FAUST had won a tennis match. It had been a LONG day. The husband, thin-moustached, wasn't amused. He was wearing designer casuals, billboard bragging. He closed his shiny-covered book, removed his noise-cancelling headphones, stood, and punched the BOHEMIAN miner to the ground. *Kazam. Kapow.*

Go on, kill me. KILL me. This was the atmosphere.

It was a question of HONOUR now that the swords were drawn. The airport terminal was suddenly a circus, the duties of witness weighing liked brotherhood upon captive passengers, whose prodigal plane had just landed. Did you know, said the woman, that Baron von Trautmonsdorf once challenged a fellow officer to a duel over a poem he'd penned which insinuated limpness of hair (and other body parts)? They were both in LOVE with the same green-eyed woman. They both died, killed by love. She married someone else. Don't you think it BEWILDERING, the offence that gentlemen take? *Thump.*

Go on, kill HER. Kill her. This was the atmosphere.

Without exception, no one at Perth Airport was related to von Trautmonsdorf or knew anything much of the HISTORY of duelling, the hundreds of thousands of lives that offended honour claimed, but of the feudal nature of the human heart, they all knew a thing or two. That, and the radical incapacity of VIOLENCE to seek sense. So when the miner rose from the floor, still stunned, he was everybody's ghost. The husband, taking no chances, hit him over the head with his book, then the woman hit out at them both with her new, laburnum-soft yellow handbag. Announcements ECHOED. Idiots, hissed the woman, hitting the men again, completely sure now that she disliked her husband, her handbag, the very idea of marriage and, especially, flying. *Sigh*.

This was the ATMOSPHERE. Please don't let me die.

Space race space race space race. Settle down you lot, some old man said. Get a GRIP. Why was everybody always flying to Melbourne? To shop? Recoiling from her undergraduate enthusiasms for displays of spite, the woman calmed down. Yeah, settle down, both men said to her. ALLIES now. She adjusted her bra. What president was it—was it Roosevelt?—she asked them, What did he answer when asked what book the Soviets might best be gifted to read of the advantages of stateside society? The SEARS CATALOGUE, he suggested. Let's go shopping boys. Her husband said, we're not going to America, why the fuck are you talking about America? Too right, said the miner, fuck America, that place is FUCKED UP. And the stout and the regular and the slender and the injured alike swiftly boarded their plane. They left some things in the TERMINAL—rigid imbecility, vatic malevolencies, stupefied endurances, wild losses—and hoped, swords sheathed, eccentrically, that they might be seated together, without restraint. *Hissssssss.*

Up in the atmospheric night sky, they saw more stars than flags or nations needed.
PLEASE DON'T DIE DON'T DIE DON'T DIE

The sonic life of tennis

That first marriage was a marmalade forest
solved eventually by a series of thwartings—
inaction, disobedience, humanity largely, the
refusal to countenance that love could be
so ideologically disappointing. So grinding.
One day I awoke, gently packed, and left.

And here I am in the country for the weekend.
It's a Saturday afternoon in a butterflied spring,
everything made of mint and joy. So sparkly.
Zippers in lazily fielded tents, laundered sheets
bewitching with their cotillion dance, laughter,
balls kissing racquets: a secret disco of bliss.

I do not care what happens next.

Debriefing | Happy

Inside my head I know more than I could possibly use, stuff like swimming carnivals and the Sex Pistols, the suffragettes and same-sex marriage, Susan Sontag, the Concorde over Putney Bridge of a Wednesday evening like a mothership and Berlin with its superb, unsolved wall. If I could tap my own telephone just to know more I would, even though what I do know is truly useless.

I'll give you fish, I'll give you candy | just give me back my man.

A cold wind comes shuddering. I'm boating on an edgeless lake with a Zeppelinesque soundscape—everything is howling. I was safe there, in the past. I know this because it has passed and I am still here, and this compounds the cherishable rather than the perishable. My boat slaps homewards across the urgent sound in soothing, forgetful bounces. Soon it will be time for the fire.

Coastal fugue

Some friends I once knew well have been separately to Antarctica. One won a prize, the other needed to paint something white. Us and our luck and our needs: nothing has changed then since high school, since Sydney in the 1980s with its garage bands and women's marches and university bars and hungover Sunday recovery meals at the Malaya when it was still by Central Station, before we all became solid. Before we snapped and dropped away, and left for our Moscows, our Londons our Byron Bays, seeping with the sap of our origins. Before, when our canvasses were as blank as ice.

An iceberg twice the size of New York is set to break away from the Antarctic ice shelf. NASA is involved, they've been spying on the Halloween crack for 35 years: it's about to meet another rift. 'Glaciologist' is a job that suburban girls with beachside minds never imagined but with our acquired brighter repertoires we know them now as the professional fortune tellers they are: sea levels will rise. Investments in coastal properties and inheritances and much else are at risk. No one mentions the planet. That's too Greenham Common.

First come the fissures, then the falling away: they call it calving, but where is the cow of a mother to blame this time? I buy a bracelet online made from ocean trash. I contact my old friends. I purchase other trinkets made of rubbish retrieved from Everest. I'm worried I won't hear back from them, and go for a swim with our teenage ghosts at Bronte in the ocean pool where we all had our first kisses, and wonder at friendship's sinking demise and that the tinfoil-joy of our frozen, young lives remains fiercely erotic, and the ocean weeps as it moves. A city with an ocean at its hemline, you can't invent such fortune.

Pink milk of my morning, you fill my bath at midnight.

Selling the surfboards

1
It doesn't matter why,
but they had to go. Before the
sun had shrugged off the night
or me my resolve, I'd zipped those
boards into their silver coffins,
slid them into the station wagon, and
telling them no lies about the morning,
or the wrenching to come, driven
to Zaks, which would not open
for hours.
                              —I slept

2
Later, the slant light brightened my
mood. One by one the boys examined
the boards, laid out on repair wracks:
touch me that tenderly and I'd die. What
beautiful things they are, brave and
firm, formerly soaked with splendour, but
dead to me now. Once, we'd travelled
the wet world together. They have
wisdom within their fibreglass,
I have cancer upon my skin, only
one of those consequences
is contagious.
                              —I wept

3
The material world, our enthusiastic
relationship to it, is necessary, it renders
godliness available to our otherwise
stupid senses. Touch this. Feel this.
Kiss this future. Want everything.

Be that largely alive, be game
to devour, to desire what you
might not deserve, but surf
it, own it, regardless, and
live, on credit.

—I'm inept

4
This is not the beginning of the going it is
the gone, and it is good. Surfshops have their
own stratospheres—smell this: the sad,
chalked perfume of board wax on land,
the gourmet bouquet of wetsuits, the ocean
stuck on human skin, the salted life that
dances in this cubed haven. Bury me here
amongst this gentle commerce,
beneath the sign above the register
that reads *no wankers*. Heaven, here in
this sparkling place. Love traded

—without debt

Glamorous discontinuum

fly me to the moon
turning away from the commune
from the 1970s
from hippie fundamentalism
from the patriarchy of lush-eyed men
from the lazy sleaze of the bourgeoisie
from the hedonic infantilism of equality
from the rudeness of democracy
from the swarm-logic of Dionysus
from rainbows and boggy mysticism
felt like kissing dead Frank Sinatra—
embarrassing: dangerous: corporate

let me play among the moon and stars
the moon was London
it was a long way from Nimbin
it was working-class
it was fundamentally aspirational
it was foreign to the desire to be level
it was the witchcraft of glam rock
it was the fascinating spell of aristocracy
it was the desire for nobility via glitter
it was crunchy guitars, bubblegum lyrics
it was outrageous theatricality, platform boots
it was Bolan and Bowie and Slade and the Sweet
it was a Suzie Q chemical rush to the future
it was men in women's clothes with velvet dreams
it was the thump of the glam descend
it was daft mystery as expressionist pap
it was music against immiseration—
Kylie Minogue was a sex worker, by comparison,
and Germaine Greer was wrong about everything,
so hold my hand, and let us sing

in other words

Afterword

Gladland is a poetic tale of what heartbreak can and can't do to a modern woman. Set to a 1970s psychosonic soundtrack, and staged in various cities from Detroit to Rome and Perth, these poems are glamrock operettas of everyday life, well-versed in its romantic absurdities and glories. As a collection, *Gladland* makes original, theoretical arguments about female desire under late capitalism, exploring love as basically a sonic memory funded by a belief in nostalgia as balm, and salvation from the otherwise irredeemable present. Poem by poem, *Gladland* dances towards a revolutionary theory of love as a key commodity of an experience economy which is in itself a trickster. The speaker—who surrenders to being a wild subject—and her actions are investigated in minute detail, revealing the difference between love and its commodification in an increasingly precarious world. A series of epistolary poems also hold to account writers who have in turn haunted the speaker, from Sylvia Plath to Robert Lowell and Dorothy Hewett. Here, confessional impulses are scrutinised as agents capable of deconstructing self from meaning and identity, and encouraging madness. Is truth still too dangerous for the female subject? A contemporary elegy, a poetic tale of praise, lament and consolation, *Gladland* speaks with tenderness and a feminist clarity to the politics of joy and sorrow that underscore the history of women's addiction to love. A philosophical and exhilarating examination of the human impulse to run away from and into trouble, this collection employs the witnessing imagination to offer testimony, reminding us equally of poetry's roar and solace, and that the personal is forever political.

Acknowledgements

Thank you to the editors and journals in which earlier versions of some of these poems were first published: *New River Press | Yearbook* 2019; *Axon*; *Grieve* 2018; *Diodata*; *LiNQ Journal*; *1over8*; *The Australian*; *Australian Poetry Journal*; *Bad Betty Press | Alter Egoes*: solidarity. Thank you to my writing colleagues at John Cabot University and Curtin University. I am indebted to the writings of the late Mark Fisher (K-Punk); Simon Reynolds (*Shock and Awe: Glam Rock and Its Legacy, from the Seventies to the Twenty-first Century*); Julian Cope (*Head-On/Repossessed)*, and above all Vivien Goldman's *Revenge of the She-Punks: A Feminist Music History from Poly Styrene to Pussy Riot*. My parents (reluctantly) sponsored my first rock concerts at the Coffs Harbour Civic Centre when I was still in primary school: Hush and Skyhooks changed my life, so thanks for that mum and dad, as well as all that 1970s parenting aka 'here's-some-money-for-the-jukebox-now-please-piss-off' and the endless 'Bohemian Rhapsody' that was Friday nights at the Plantation Hotel. I should also admit that I wrote my first poem listening to their ABBA LPs, and my first good one making it through high school listening to The Saints, and other records gifted by friends. Thank you all for that radical education of the mind and heart. Thanks too to *On The Street* in Sydney and *LAM* in London for all the breaks you gave a young journalist. Basically, thank you for the music, and the lessons in love.

And to James, who always knows what record to play, thank you most of all.

About the author

Susan Bradley Smith was born in Bega in 1963 and attended school and university in New South Wales. After working as a rock journalist in Sydney and London in the 1980s, she commenced an academic career, and has since published widely as a creative writer and historian. Her books include the memoir *Friday Forever*, the verse novel *The Postcult Heart*, and the suffrage theatre history, *A Splendid Adventure*. Susan teaches at Curtin University in Perth.

www.ingramcontent.com/pod-product-compliance
Lightning Source LLC
Chambersburg PA
CBHW020331010526
44107CB00054B/2067